Addicted to my Couch

Addicted to my Couch

Dr. Linda Fisher

Library of Congress Control Number: 2019904181
ISBN: Hardcover   978-1-7960-2662-7
                 Softcover   978-1-7960-2663-4
                 eBook   978-1-7960-2666-5

Print information available on the last page.

Rev. date: 04/10/2019

To order additional copies of this book, contact:
Xlibris
1-888-795-4274
www.Xlibris.com
Orders@Xlibris.com
794287

Contents

DEDICATION

THERE ARE SO many people that need to be included in the dedication to this book. All are equally important, and all have kept me balanced, encouraged, and moving forward. The impetus for this book really comes from my brother, Lt. Col. Randy G. Fisher. He was not only my brother but also a father, a husband, a son, a friend, and my hero. Most importantly, he was a man of God, so I have the peace that comes with knowing I will see him again.

My friends and family have encouraged me and never gave up on my ability to accomplish anything. I appreciate their sacrifices and continuing support. My two best friends provided unending support and friendship that mean more than I can ever explain.

Matt Sloane, Sanjay Gupta, and the Fit Nation team–my life has been changed forever due to the idea of the Fit Nation Challenge, a moment in my life I will never forget but relish and forever be grateful.

Finally, I dedicate this to those that need the support and encouragement to take control of their lives and make a change to live life instead of letting it pass by. Our moments are precious; set the bar higher than you can reach, and then reach it anyway! I hope you find strength and encouragement in the pages to follow.

Addicted to my Couch

A Story about Tragedy, Motivation, Inspiration and Success

PREFACE

We are all sent a series of great opportunities
brilliantly disguised as impossible situations.

—Unknown

HOW DOES AN overachiever become an underachiever? How do you no longer meet the expectations of those around you, let alone stop meeting your own expectations? *Overachiever* has often been the term used to describe me in every aspect of my life. I was always busy, always active, and always accomplishing those tasks that seemed outside what was possible for most. One day everything changed.

This book is the story of my "couch addiction." It is the story of how I got there, how I made the decision to change my life, and the steps I took to effect change. This story is true. It is about challenges, small victories, setbacks, motivation, and success; but mostly, it is about taking control of your life and living. I hope I can help anyone who reads this find th e motivation and inspiration to change their life and the courage to move forward.

INTRODUCTION

THIS BOOK IS about my addiction to my couch, how I got there, and the steps I used to get off the couch. Couch addiction is the inability to live or enjoy life, even the inability to move. The cause can be physical, mental, or a combination of both. It is when events overcome our lives and stop us from moving forward. I use the term *couch addiction* metaphorically to describe those people that have lost their zest for life. Whether the events are intentional or unintentional, one day you find yourself sitting inside your home, wondering why your life will not change. I was one of those people for nearly four years. I hope the pages that follow will help you change your life as I have done with mine.

There is no passion to be found playing small . . . in settling
for a life that is less than the one you are capable of living.

–Nelson Mandela

This book is intended to inspire and motivate anyone who makes the decision to change their life. Part of motivating you is giving you my story, a little history, and the events that led to my downward spiral as well as the steps and events that brought me back to life. However, I will tell you now that taking your life back is a lifelong journey for any one. My goal is to continue moving forward and helping you, or anyone who will listen, move forward as well. There is a monumental difference between surviving life and living life in the moment. Now I know the difference; I want to share information with anyone that will listen!

CHAPTER 1

Every Climb Starts at the Base of the Mountain

Strength and growth come only through

continuous effort and struggle.

–Napoleon Hill

B Y READING THIS book, you have taken the first step toward making a change. You will find I am very honest about my plight, and this honesty has given me the ability to move out of feeling ashamed and move forward to being proud of myself. My accomplishments are far short of miraculous, but what I have discovered is that all accomplishments are important. Many people fail to see the importance of all successes, big or small. If we are moving forward, we are moving in the right direction.

Without going into too much of a life history, my story briefly starts at age twelve. Since that age, I knew I wanted to be a police officer. I saw this as an important job that was noble and honest. At this age, I knew I would have to decide my own path and dedicate myself to that path if I wanted to be successful. This is exactly what I did. I knew I would need an education but could not pay for college. I was a good athlete who had a real gift for basketball. My goal was to go to college on a basketball scholarship.

Everyone from town said I would never get there–I was not good enough; I was from too small of a town. Everyone told me it could not happen, it would not happen, etc. I never used to listen when people told me "You can't," "You won't," or "It is beyond your abilities." Actually, these statements fueled my fire to prove that I could. I worked hard and practiced for hours before and after school every day during my senior year.

Then the offers came. Eight division 1 full-ride scholarships and forty-four small school offers. I was the first full-ride division 1 athlete, male or female, from Bend

Senior High. I won the Wade Trophy for scoring more than one thousand points during my high school career and many other awards. You got it–I spent the next four years playing college basketball at Washington State University, where I also scored over one thousand points.

Fast-forward several years, and my dream as a twelve-year-old had come true. I was one of five women working for the Eugene Police Department as a police officer. Receiving my badge was one of the greatest moments of my life. This was the job, career, and life for me. I was able to take my passion and make it a career, all the while looking for every opportunity to make the world a little better, one person or one situation at a time.

Fast-forward several more years, and I am a lieutenant in charge of patrol operations at a medium-sized municipal agency. Patrol was always my passion and the part of police work I really enjoyed. I always knew I was going to be chief some day and focused all my efforts on achieving this goal.

But in one afternoon, my life changed forever. It was not just one event but a myriad of events that started my life cascading into a downward spiral. These are the events that led me to the couch and in need of a plan for recovery. One afternoon, I was driving to a nearby department store to pick up some items for the evidence room. One moment, I was driving along; and the next moment, I slammed broadside into a car that ran the stop sign in front of me. I shoved my right foot down on the brake as hard as I could, but there was no way to avoid the impending crash. As my foot pressed down on the brake pedal, the impact jerked the car to the left, snapping my hip to the right.

Once the cars came to a stop, it was quiet, and the dust began to settle. I did a quick mental self-assessment, and everything felt fine. I was able to get out of my car and make sure the driver of the other vehicle was okay. I did not go to the emergency room, I did not hit my head; I did not require stitches—nothing that dramatic. Since I didn't suffer any cuts or bruises and I didn't hit my head, I decided the accident did not require a trip to the emergency room. However, my back and hip really hurt, and I could feel where I was going to be bruised from the seat belt, which had provided safety by holding me in my seat. A few days later, I was physically unable to move off my couch. I could not sit, I could barely walk, and I could hardly move. The only thing I could do was lie on my back . . . and the pain was unbearable. Next came the trip to the emergency room.

The prognosis: my hip was damaged, and I had three herniated (or bulging) discs in my back. The next two years were filled with physical therapy, rehabilitation, injections, and unsurprisingly, weight gain. Along with the multiple visits to the doctor, there was also a lot of self-pity. I went to work on light duty, which meant I could not wear a uniform or patrol the city. For the most part, my spirits were good, and I knew it was just a matter of time before I would be back to full duty doing the job I loved. It never occurred to me that my lifelong career would be coming to an end. When I did not improve, I went to an orthopedic surgeon who specialized in spines. He simply said, "You will never be a police officer again." Three surgeons and two second opinions later, there was a recurring theme I would not be able to return to working on the road as a police officer.

Many things went through my head, but mainly, What will I do if I cannot be a police officer? It had never occurred to me that this would ever happen. Well, it did, and I found myself medically retired at the age of forty-three after nineteen years of law enforcement and a blossoming career that withered up and died. This may not seem like such a big deal for many, but law enforcement was my purpose in life–a passion so strong that much of my identity was wrapped up in the job. I strongly believed in the job and helping others. I had dedicated my life to being the best officer I could be and never considered any other profession.

Losing my career began my downward spiral, and before I knew it, my life had become a vicious cycle. Many of the people I worked with were people I trusted with my life. Due to the situations that officers are often faced with, there is a special bond that is built in the law enforcement community. There are situations that officers are placed in that many do not understand. You are exposed to the ugliest and worst circumstances of human nature, many of these situations others just can't possibly understand. You really see the ugliest aspects of society, with periodic positive signs of humanity. The experiences of policing change one's perspective on people and society. Once I left the department, I felt like an outsider and that there was no one who could truly understand what I was going through. It took a long time to come to grips with the reality that I had lost my career, the job I had always dreamed about.

Jumping ahead for just a minute, in May 2010, I had the opportunity to ride bikes with Lance Armstrong. Having read Lance's book *It's Not About the Bike,* I knew he had been faced with losing his longtime passion of cycling. While on a training ride in Texas, I gave Lance a brief scenario of what had happened in my life, and I formed the big question "What do you do?" How do you move forward when it seems like everything that mattered was outside of your reach?

Lance and I discussed the different personalities of people. For example, there are people who are passionate about everything they do, and whenever they do something, they are all in. The all-in people are the Monica Gellers (*Friends*) and the Tom Bradys of the world, the people that climb the highest mountain peaks then look out over the horizon to see if there just might be another mountain a little taller and a little more challenging. Everything they do is heartfelt, important, and the goal is to be successful, if not the best.

On another hand, there are people who care about doing a good job and how well they perform, but performance alone is not their priority. These people can do well at many things, but do not excel to being great at any one particular skill. These are the slow-and-steady performers that you can always count on–the sixth man or the inspirational best friend. (The team would not exist without these type of people.) For them, coming in second is not the devastation that it can be to the all-ins. If the truly passionate personality is an A-plus, this person is a B-plus performer–definitely above average but doesn't make the headlines.

Finally, there are those who go through life without any real investment in anything. They function fine and have many interests but are not truly passionate about anything. For these people, if they lost a career, they would move on to something else with relative ease. These people are necessary in almost everything. Not everyone is going to be an A-plus performer or have the drive to show up everyday and give 100 percent. They are fairly indifferent in terms of what they enjoy and have an interest in many things, but no one thing is more important than the other. Life is smooth and laid back. They have no real winning titles and no real concerns about anything. I see someone from this category as a C-plus performer, above average but very content to stay where they stand. They see no need to be at the end of the line but no reason to be in front either.

There is nothing negative about any of these groups. This is just my way of drawing a picture of the different types of people I see and where I fit into the scheme. Sometimes I think it would be nice to be content where I am standing at any given moment, but that is just not who I am.

I fall into the category of *all-ins*, people who are passionate about everything they do. The *all-in* people can be devastated by loss, and I found myself inconsolable regarding the loss of my career as a police officer. For passionate people who suffer loss, if they do not find a new passion, they will spend the rest of their lives like a dog chasing their tail.

Lance had the Livestrong Foundation, and he has been all in since it started. I am still trying to find a new passion to replace the old one, but I have to admit, the time I spent on the couch thinking about the *what-ifs* was equivalent to running around in circles. I was wasting a lot of time and energy while accomplishing nothing. I think the loss can be hard on anyone, especially when it was an event you had no control of. The A-plus performers have a desire to be in control of their own destiny. How do you prepare to lose what you believe to be your destiny?

A few months after being medically retired, I was home in bed when I got the call that only seemed to bolster my addiction to the couch. My brother had been in a serious motor vehicle crash. When I called my sister-in-law, she was crying, and she told me "Linda, it's really bad." A frightening feeling came over me, and I knew in an instant that my brother was not going to live. I knew it because I felt it, and I absolutely knew I had to get my family prepared. I had to get my mother and let my other brother and sister know what had happened. My brother and I had discussed the possibility of my being killed in the line of duty. The department was to call my brother, and he was to tell my mother. It had never occurred to me that I would be notifying my mother of my brother's death. My brother Lt. Col. Randy Fisher passed away on October 1, 2006, six days after the car crash, due to the severe injuries.

I do not even think I can explain the loss of my brother– not then and not now. The impact of his loss is still difficult to quantify. His loss had a dramatic impact on my life and was a critical element in my continued couch addiction. It seemed that losing my career and my brother in a three-month period was the nail in the coffin as far as my being in a permanent state of couch addiction was concerned. Could it get any worse?

Yet it did get worse. About three months later, my step-grandmother passed away. Next, my sister in law was diagnosed with cancer on Thanksgiving and died in January just a few months later. This was followed by the death of my mother and father-in-law. Next was the passing of my father after a massive heart attack on the anniversary of my brother's death. I thought, *How could one person bear this much pain, loss, and suffering?* The loss of my career, health, and family left me addicted to my couch and looking down a gallon tub of ice cream. It was as if I was actually superglued to the couch. There was no motivation, no energy, and no passion. I would just sit on my couch, motionless as my life passed by. At times, I would wallow in the bad luck that was my life while waiting for my life to magically change and believing it would with no effort on my part.

Looking back, the biggest impact on me was the loss of my brother. It took me several years to really understand the depth of the loss, and I'm not even sure that I grasp it now. My father had such difficulty with my brother's death and somehow felt it was his fault. I was not surprised at my dad's passing; however, my pain was no less—and possibly more for the fact he passed on the anniversary of my brother's death. This only served to cement my couch addiction to a permanent state.

Thought for the Chapter

I will share an encompassing thought at the end of every chapter—a thought you can take with you to help make the journey of recovery easy to remember and a step-by-step process. Not every thought will apply to every person, but they are important steps to recovery and deserve consideration.

As I experienced these different events and misfortunes in my life, I could only think to myself, *Misery certainly loves company.* We will draw others into our misery and demand that they feel our pain and misfortune. If they choose to be around us, then they have to be miserable too. People in misery have no time for happy people to stop their negative mojo. How can you tell me that my pain will pass? We convince ourselves and try to convince others that we cannot change our lives. It is much easier to sit and do nothing when you feel others understand your decision to quit life and offer support. This leads us to believe that what we have (sitting on our couch in misery) is all there is, that it is our new normal. Just like that, our life moves to the dark side, and we allow it too.

CHAPTER 2

Call It What You Want

Happiness is not a matter of intensity but of
balance, order, rhythm and harmony.

–Thomas Merton

MENTAL HEALTH PROFESSIONALS would tell you I was struggling with clinical depression. Some would say that I was mourning. Many would say that I was in a mental health crisis or just feeling sorry for myself. I refer to this time in my life as the "black hole." I was living in a black hole, and within it, I became lost. Whatever term you want to attach to this experience, I saw this as the start to my couch addiction.

I want to talk about the *black hole* a little more because I am certain there are many people who have experienced this or may be experiencing this same situation now. It is not so much that the world is dark as there is an experience and sense of being totally lost. In this darkness, there is no direction; you do not know which way to go or what to do. There are times you know you need to make a change, but you are too lost to figure out how to make that change or fathom what the change would look like. Even worse, I was afraid to even want to change. I felt safe in the darkness. The black hole kept me in a state of paralysis, and the results were that I lost my spirit and my drive to be anything.

I came to a better understanding of the term *couch addiction* when I began to go through my recovery stage and I began to change my life. As I mentioned earlier, the term *couch addiction* is a metaphor. However, I use *couch addiction* as a framework for determining where one needs to start the process to regain or reclaim one's life—or how I used it to reclaim my life. I also like to use the couch addiction metaphor because if you have found yourself in this position, you are going to be in a constant state of struggle internally, fighting to prevent yourself from returning to the couch. If you are familiar with an alcoholic in sobriety, know that they are in a constant state of fighting the desire to drink. Similarly with the couch addiction, there is a constant fight to stay off the couch but a seductive draw internally to bring you back.

There might still be room to debate whether you need to hit rock bottom to make the decision to get your life back. I am not a counselor or a psychologist, but I don't believe you need to hit rock bottom before making a change. You just need to make a decision to make a change. Remember, change is difficult for everyone, not just you. I think you just need to be tired of where you are. For me, I became tired of watching life go by while I did nothing to break free or make a change. For you the circumstances may be different, but I will tell you this with absolute certainty: the black hole will suck you in and slowly suffocate the life out of you.

Here is my question to you: are you spending day after day, weekend after weekend, or hour after hour sitting inside your house trying to make the decision to get your life back? I certainly think people end up in the couch addiction situation through circumstances that happened in their lives and by their choices. I did not choose to lose my career. I did not choose to lose my brother. I am not even sure I chose to be on the couch while life passed me by. However, it came about. It is where I ended up, and it could have been where I stayed. As I sat in the depth of my couch addition, the black hole became deeper and deeper until I wasn't even sure I could climb out. The responsibility was mine to make a change or stay where I sat. This choice is yours as well. Are you going to stay on the couch or are you going to make a change? I have always felt that we need to be accountable for our actions and behaviors. It is one thing to survive life; it is something else to thrive in it. Is this where you are, or is this a question you have asked yourself? Only you can change your life. If you are addicted to your couch, you have to make the decision to make a change. No one is going to make that change for you. It has to come from deep within yourself.

Thought for the Chapter

Accountability is an important part of the recovery process. Holding yourself accountable for your day-to-day activities is critical. This does not mean that you meet every goal but that you are moving forward toward them. Look for people around you who will be supportive of your every effort no matter how big or small. Recognize that baby steps are important, along with recognizing small victories. It is important that you set small reasonable goals and then follow through. It is just as important that you recognize your successes as you have spent so much time recognizing your failures. It is really easy to discount the "small" steps of success. These may be your most important steps, as these are steps for you, your growth, and your successes–don't minimize them!

CHAPTER 3

The Decision to Change

It is not the strongest of the species that survives,
nor the most intelligent that survives. It is the
one that is most adaptable to change.

–Charles Darwin

I WAS HOME ONE evening, feeding my couch addiction. This was not a special day since sitting on my couch and wallowing in self-pity had become a daily occurrence. However, on this day, I decided to watch *a popular weight-loss program.* I had been addicted to my couch for about three years. I was easily seventy-five pounds overweight, waiting for my world to magically change but not wanting to do anything about it. Even though I had heard about the show through advertisements, I had never seen the show before. I thought it was a game show and refused to watch it. I believed the show was designed to exploit the weaknesses of others, which I did not think should be television-worthy. I had also given myself the "loser" title, and how dare they use it! I had become the ultimate loser in my own mind. Up to this point, I had no idea what the show was really about.

When the show came on, I was suddenly watching heartfelt interviews with people who were overweight to the point it was life-threatening. Some people had tragedies in their lives that had led them to their weight problems, while others experienced weight problems their entire lives. As I watched the show, I did not hear what was being said as much as being delighted in how hard the workouts were. In my mind, there was no relationship between the contestants and myself. I actually saw myself as a hard-assed trainer pushing people until they puked, cried, or gave up and not as a contestant in need of change.

The next week, I watched the show, this time intentionally. I ate ice cream while I watched the show, thinking *I could do these workouts* as the contestants were struggling through. I laughed to myself that I was eating ice cream while they sweated, complained, vomited, and sometimes quit. I thought, *If anyone yelled at me like that, I would kick their ass, and I would never quit* (when actually I had quit a long time ago!).

The next time I watched the show, I no longer laughed at the workouts. I heard more of the heartfelt testimonies of ordinary people–ordinary people who had found the courage to change their lives by going on the show, undertaking grueling workouts, and rebuilding their lives one day at a time. I thought, *I have two options. I can gain thirty more pounds and try to go on the show, or I can make the decision to change my life now.* Many of the people on the show had a physical life-threatening illness, obesity.

In my mind, there is no doubt that being addicted to your couch is or can become a life-threatening illness. I watched the show with a renewed interest in what the contestants and trainers were saying. I began to see a connection between the contestants' situations and mine. The bottom line was, many of these people had given up on their lives. The only difference was that they were eating their way through. I had gained weight, but it was mostly due to inactivity after years of being active. However, the outcome was inevitably the same: we had quit living life and became addicted to a lifestyle of nothing.

Thought for the Chapter

It took a few weeks to *start* making the needed life changes. I did not jump up and get on the treadmill, join a gym, or start dieting. I am going to talk later in this book about giving yourself credit for all victories, big or small. Making a decision to change your life is a victory; starting to make the actual change is another victory. Beating an addiction is a process. It takes time, and it takes baby steps. That is why I have chosen to use addiction as my metaphor, and rehabilitation is a process.

CHAPTER 4

"Going to Rehab"—the Decision to Get Off the Couch

Sometimes the most interesting destinations
have no path. Be willing to explore.

—Unknown

S O HERE IS another point for those people wanting to change their lives. Looking at the big picture is too overwhelming, so setting small realistic goals will help you accomplish anything you set your mind to and build your confidence along the way. The end goal is important, but the journey is where you are going to learn the most about yourself as well as learn and experience success.

I had to be realistic about my physical condition. I was overweight, and I had a bad back, a bad hip, and a lot of chronic pain. But there was an emotional component to my condition as well. I was in my black hole. The emotional pain of losing my brother and several other family members in a very short period had left me numb.

I spent so much time doing nothing but being addicted to my couch I had a hard time sleeping. Over the next month or so, I watched too many infomercials. I had diet plans coming in the mail, exercise equipment, self-help books—you name it, I ordered it! *GIMMICKS ARE NOT GOING TO HELP YOU GET OFF THE COUCH! It's going to take a lot of hard work.* Also, changing your life is a journey, not a trip to the convenience store. Making this type of change is a life revolution and requires that you make a commitment to the transformation in the long term.

It would have been easy to stay on the couch, but I decided then I had to make a change. (I would recommend consulting your doctor if you are getting ready to make physical and diet changes). From the time I decided to make the change and the time I started making the change, it was a couple of weeks, but I kept telling myself, "Remember, it's the small step of success." (Trying to make giant steps is all too often overwhelming.)

I had reached a point of disgust with what I had become, a couch addict. The disgust had hindered my goal more then it motivated me. I reached the stage where I knew I had to do something about it, but I still needed to shake that feeling of self-pity. If we find ourselves having a pity party, we will find that wallowing in pity seems like the best thing to do in the moment. So I say, *change the moment*. Words like *pitifuly*, *disgusting*, and *shameful* are all adjectives that will prevent recovery. These words should have no place in your vocabulary. Throw those words away now and never pick them back up.

I was realistic about my limitations and knew I would have to make small and smart changes about changing my life. At first, I had big plans: I was going to get fit, go back to police work, do this, do that . . . And the list went on and on. This became overwhelming, and in no time, I had given up and was back spending time on the couch doing nothing but thinking about change. Thinking about change is a place to start but *does not* lead to actual change. You have to do more than think about change. Eventually you need to implement change.

After thinking things through, I thought I needed to get at least twenty-five pounds off before I started any kind of exercise. I thought if I can get the weight off, I could start to exercise with minimal pain. I would start feeling better on the inside and exercise would be less painful. The other thought was I would need to strengthen my core (abdominal muscles) to protect my back before I could do any real exercise. I also thought strengthening my core would help minimize my pain. I was very focused on minimizing my physical pain and had no idea how much this would positively impact my emotional pain.

Finally, it came down to eating the right things in the right amount–sticking to a diet, making a plan in regards to food and determining what are the right things to eat. Within a few months, I had lost twenty-five pounds. This had been my weight-loss goal to trigger the start to my exercising. I started using my elliptical machine everyday and worked my way up to one thousand sit-ups a week. An important point in this paragraph is the plan. When I hit the weight-loss goal, I started the next phase, exercise.

Thought for the Chapter

Figure out a plan and stick to it. If you don't have a plan, it is difficult to tell what strides you are making and if you are headed in the right direction. If you don't have a plan, this will lead to stress, indecision, and failure. It is okay to change your plan, but be certain to have one. I will delve more into how to make an effective plan of action. However, I think it is imperative to understand that making a plan is important because this is where the real-life change begins. Here is an important tip: nothing about the months covered in this chapter was easy. I had good moments and bad moments. There were times when I ate things I should not have and times when I did nothing but return to sitting on the couch. There were times when I asked, "What's the point?" I quit a few times, had several days in a row with no exercise, and the words I mentioned earlier–*pity*, *disgust*, and *embarrassment*– came back into my vocabulary. However, in imparting my wisdom to you, make this your mantra when these moments come: "Remember, this is a journey, not a trip."

CHAPTER 5

The Challenge

An old day passes, a new day arrives. The important thing is to make it meaningful: a meaningful friend or a meaningful day.

–Dalai Lama

I HAD BEEN WORKING my self-designed exercise program fairly well to this point. I had found some success in weight loss, was starting to have less pain, and was proud of myself for what I had accomplished. Slowly, I began building confidence. A friend of mine sent me a web link to CNN's health page with a note stating, "Do you think you could do this?" I looked at the link. CNN's Fit Nation was looking for five people (which later turned out to be six) to compete in the New York City Triathlon. I thought, *Sure, I can do that!* The link mentioned that the contestant needed to send in a video as to why that person should be chosen to take the Fit Nation Challenge and change his or her life.

A week or so went by, and my friend asked if I was going to apply for the challenge. I thought, *Why would they pick me?* My friend insisted I had a story to tell and encouraged me daily to put in my application for the contest. I thought there was no chance I would ever be chosen. However, it was apparent my friend was not going to leave me alone until I submitted the video. I reluctantly made my video and told my story.

The story was the same story I mentioned here. I mentioned how I had found myself in a tough place, but I had decided about six months ago to change my life. With the challenges I had faced and with this newfound determination to change my circumstances, I stated that was why I should be chosen for the challenge. I also mentioned that being chosen for the challenge would also be a continuation of my life change.

The week before Christmas, I received a call. When I answered the phone, it was CNN. The CNN producer, Matt

Sloane, was calling to tell me I would be flying to New York in January as part of the Fit Nation Challenge. I thought, *Holy crap!*

Two weeks later, I was on my way to New York City. I flew to New York and met the CNN crew, trainer, and the other participants. The entire experience was amazing. In many ways, the next six months were a whirlwind. When I left New York, I thought, *What did I get myself into?* On the other hand, I thought, *What a great way to be accountable!* Five other people were there with similar circumstances, all facing the same challenge I would soon be facing.

There is a key component to this part of the story: accountability. It is important to have others to help keep you accountable. For me, I knew that the Fit Nation Challenge would help keep me accountable. For you, it is important to find a support system that will help keep you accountable. Whether it is someone to work out with, someone conscientious about diet, or whatever the task or program is that will help you recover. So here is a note about accountability: nobody likes to get called out, so find ways to keep yourself accountable. Accountability is an important step in the process of recovery.

Everyone in the CNN Fit Nation group had a story to tell. As I heard their various stories, I recognized that they too had experienced their "black holes." They shared how they had reached a point where they recognized they had to make some change in their lives or they would be forever addicted to their couch (my thoughts). Their stories inspired and encouraged me. I recognized I was not alone. So I shared my story as well. As I did this, I realized that I was encouraging them, which in turn helped encourage me. We formed a close bond, and the group talked on the phone weekly. This also helped with the level of accountability, since we were letting everyone know what we were doing.

Thought for the Chapter

Accountability is important for many reasons. First, when you are at a point like I was, you have no accountability for yourself. I had lost all personal expectations. I did not expect anything out of myself, and I thought no one else expected anything from me, so what did it matter if I accomplished anything? Accountability is the way to change this negative thought process that goes on inside us. We all have something to contribute, and it is important that we all do contribute.

Part of recovery is changing the way you think and realizing that you have a lot of important contributions to make.

Through the process of training with Fit Nation, I not only had accountability toward the rest of the group and CNN, but I began to develop accountability to myself. I have to say that the accountability toward the group to help them be successful came first. Then holding myself accountable and developing expectations for myself came next. Over time, accountability has allowed me to continue to move forward.

CHAPTER 6

Two Steps Forward and One Step Back—Establish a Mind-Set for Success

Only those who will risk going too far can possibly find out how far one can go.

–T. S. Eliot

WHEN I FIRST got back from New York, I was almost in shock. I had met such amazing people and some celebrities that supported and valued the Fit Nation lifestyle. The people we had met in New York genuinely seemed to care about getting all of us on the right track. Being in New

York, meeting everyone, training . . . It all made the triathlon and my commitment a reality. In six months, I would be swimming a mile in the Hudson River, biking 25 miles down the West Side Highway, and running 6.2 miles through the Harlem Hills in Central Park.

The thought of all of this was completely overwhelming, and I think I had mentally quit before I even started. By the time I got home, I had convinced myself I could never complete the challenge. There was my couch again. I ended up on my couch, wondering how I could get out of the commitment. After all, what was I thinking? After a few days, I encouraged myself to go swim. I had done some swimming during my physical therapy from the car crash, so I might as well start there. One thing led to another, and I found myself moving forward. I rode my bike about six miles one day, I would swim for fifteen to twenty minutes another day, and then run a mile in between.

This process was slow, and I had to really convince myself to take the smallest of steps. It would seem like every step forward led me to a step backward. You would think my confidence would improve with each small step, but instead, there was a constant struggle. I was mentally beating myself up where I would quit some of my workouts before I completed them.

Fortunately, CNN set me up with a trainer, Richard Earle. He was an amazing inspiration, and though I know I caused him frustration at times, he stuck out the next six months with me for the good, the bad, and the ugly. His continued support is one of the reasons I was able to complete the challenge. It almost seemed like he was telepathic, as he could tell when I was struggling. I would get an email or phone call from him. Essentially, he was holding me accountable. Over time, my steps forward outnumbered my steps backward. This does not mean I no longer have any steps backward, but they have become fewer and their impact is less and less.

What do I mean by "two steps forward and one step back"? It seemed I would really be making strides in my training, then I would have an overwhelming desire to quit. That sense of being on the precipice of the black hole would rear its ugly head. I would wake up one day with a bad attitude–what I call "the couch attitude"–and I would not work out. One day would turn into two then three. On two different occasions, I quit for a week. I think this is an important and valuable point. It is good to acknowledge your struggles and recognize your roadblocks. If you don't do this, then you won't know what the problems are, you can't address them, and you won't move forward. I did not learn until months into my training. I am telling you, there will be roadblocks. Expect them, and prepare to navigate around them.

Success is a mind-set. I know this probably seems obvious to a lot of people, and it did to me at one time in my life. In the times before my "black hole" experience, I had always been success oriented and knew exactly what it took to accomplish goals. I had lost this ability to have a mind-set for success. I had developed a mind-set of being lost, a mind-set of pity, anger, and frustration . . . I hadn't thought about what it took to be successful for quite some time.

One of the lessons I learned during my own struggles—and one I would like to share—is that you will need to work on changing your mind-set constantly, and I do mean constantly. It starts out with moments, hours, and then days. Success should also be the focus of your workouts. Part of that success is understanding and acknowledging that every day is a constant struggle to stay on track. This is something I still have to work on every day. I will elaborate on this further in the book. The main point is that one has to develop a mind-set for success.

Thought for the Chapter

It can be difficult to set a mind-set for success if you are not necessarily sure what success is. Part of success is recognizing small victories and all victories. On those days when you absolutely do not want to train, train anyway. Just make the workout easier or shorter. You will feel better for getting it done. The goal is not to push yourself so hard that you give up.

There is a fine line between pushing yourself forward and pushing yourself backward. You want to end this day with a step forward and not a step back–these are the days of baby steps. At this stage, I think people are still vulnerable to moving backward instead of forward and sometimes even landing back on the couch. I knew I was very vulnerable to falling back into old habits. That is why it is very important to understand that there are going to be setbacks. Expect them, and then move through them.

CHAPTER 7

You Need to Leave a Mark

There are powers inside of you which, if you could discover and use, would make of you everything you ever dreamed or imagined you could become.

—Orison Swett Marden

IT'S NOT WHAT you think; it is about leaving a mark in your mind—a mark that says you can do it, that says you can change. You make this mark every time you accomplish your goal for the day. These goals include eating right, working out, getting out of the house—anything that is a step forward and a step away from the couch. Remember these moments so you can come back and look at them later. Tell yourself, "I can do this." It might be helpful to use a journal to write down your victories and struggles, but place an asterisk besides the victories so you can come back and look at them whenever you need.

Again, feeling a disconnect between the last paragraph and this one, I am not suggesting everyone has to do a triathlon. That is just what started my recovery. However, in leaving a mark in my mind, I find the medals from my races are a great tool. I place photos of these medals around my office to serve as inspiration. I have the medals from the races, T-shirts, and other memorabilia. When I am having a day that it is more conducive to the couch life than my life of aspiration, I look at the reminders of what I have accomplished. These things are important to help remind you how far you have come and that you have the ability to keep moving forward.

Thought for the Chapter

The thought for this chapter is easy: *leave a mark*. This is a reminder for you that you can do it–that you have made changes in your life and you are capable of so much more. The changes you have made are going to be a lifetime of changes. Give yourself credit for the things you have accomplished and will accomplish. By having things around to remind you, it will help prevent a relapse. Remember, there are two ways to look at the new path in your life: Think of yourself as a wagon traveling up a hill. You are either slowly moving up the hill (success) or rolling down the hill at a high rate of speed (relapse leading to failure). This is how addiction works. It is an illness that constantly tries and sucks you back to failure. Be prepared that your couch addiction will be a continuing battle–you are either slowly moving up the hill or sliding back down at a high rate of speed.

CHAPTER 8

Race Day

*Sometimes a little pain will help us gain more than
we ever imagined. Be willing to push a little bit. The
reward will be more than you ever imagined.*

–Anonymous

WELL, I MADE it through the six months of training. I had some muscle injuries and at times had to slow down on my training along the way. I was excited to fly to New York but was scared at the same time. You definitely question yourself about training enough. Not only did I ask

"Was my training enough?" but I also asked "Could I actually do the triathlon?" Swimming in the Hudson River seemed like an impossible task. I really planned on finishing in under three hours, or at least I believed I could. I certainly thought I would be competitive.

As the race grew closer, I became more and more nervous about the Hudson River. The group went out to the starting line of the race with CNN the day before the triathlon for interviews. The water was even more disgusting than I could have imagined. It stunk so badly I wanted to dry-heave. As I looked at the water, there were dead fish, dead birds, and other things I hoped were dead floating around. It was truly the dirtiest moving water I had ever seen in my life. The smell I will never forget. I thought for sure I would vomit when I got into the water, because it was all I could do not to vomit standing next to it. Everyone was teasing me about swimming in the Hudson. I just thought, *How will I ever?*

Race day was here, and of course it started with the Hudson. I talked to myself all night and all morning. Accountability came into my mind–accountability to CNN, the group, and myself. Leaving a mark, mind-set of success, baby steps, or small goals were all thoughts that came to my mind. I encouraged myself: "It is only twenty minutes. Put your head down and go."

So that is exactly what I did. I jumped into the nasty water with approximately ninety-nine others for our starting heat. The smell was even worse while sitting in the water, but you know, I did it. I put my head down and started one stroke at a time. I touched *things* while swimming. I do not even want to know what those things were! I drank the water (accidentally) while swimming. The water was fairly rough, so it was inevitable water would get into my mouth when I turned my head to take a breath.

I kept myself calm, took one stroke at a time, and before I knew it, I was at the end. I had conquered the Hudson! Other than the big black ring of oil and dirt around my mouth and the mouths of the other competitors, it was not so bad. I had taken in a lot of water though, and for those of you that do not know, the Hudson is salt water. I knew this was going to cause some problems for me down the road.

I ran the seven-tenths of a mile to the transition area in my bare feet and in my wet suit. I wiped my face off first thing and got ready for the bike ride. I was feeling pretty good. I had one person on the CNN team to catch. He had gotten out of the water a few minutes ahead of me. I remember feeling great on my bike. I was pedaling fast and smooth and was in the groove, passing people constantly as I traveled down the West Side Highway.

A few miles into the ride, my stomach became upset. I knew it was the salt water. I drank some of my water and continued to push the bike. As I reached mile 12, there was no more pushing. I had to stop and vomit. I pulled over and started vomiting more violently than I ever remember in my lifetime. The things coming out of my mouth were definitely nothing I had eaten but more like things from the Hudson. It seemed I could not stop, and I vomited for a good ten minutes. I got back on my bike, biked a few more miles, and began vomiting again. This was it for me. I was ready to throw in the towel.

The challenge was too hard–the vomiting, the heat . . . all of it. My couch attitude was back just like that. This easily became my first sign of adversity. I thought, *Everyone will understand. I am sick. If people saw how hard I was vomiting, they would certainly understand.* My mind was working hard at convincing me not to finish the race. *I could sit here and wait for someone from the race to pick me up and bring me in. I've done the best I could.*

I realized this was not what I wanted–quitting, even though it sounded appealing. I started encouraging myself with baby steps. *Just bike slowly. Go a mile and see how you feel.* Then I started setting benchmarks (baby steps) like *Get to the overpass, Get to the top of the hill,* and *Get to the turnaround.* Finally, I told myself, *Just get back to the transition* [this is the area where you change from one event to the next, swim-bike-run], *you do not have to run.* So I did. I got back to the transition. It was not a pretty race. It was not a fast race. But I got back to the transition.

Once I was back to the transition, I took my time putting my bike away and preparing for the run. I grabbed some water and decided to walk the first mile. I thought, *Walk a mile and see how you feel.* One thing nice about the run is that there is an aid station every mile. After walking the first mile, I started to run and immediately became sick. I thought, I will walk a couple miles, then I will start to run. As soon as I would start to run, I would instantly start to get sick and return to walking. My attitude really sucked now; I just wanted to quit.

I continued walking. Eventually I would walk up the hill then run down it. I did this for the remainder of the race, with the exception that I ran the entire last mile. Finally, I was finished, I had done it–I completed the race. But something important happened here. I was so disappointed in my performance. I did not feel any enjoyment by completing the race. It was not until a few weeks later that I really thought about what I had accomplished. *Six months ago, I was addicted to my couch. Today, I am a triathlete.* It is so important to recognize victories and give them the credit they deserve. Give yourself the credit you deserve.

Thought for the Chapter

There is a lot of information about the race in this chapter. You can see the many points of success I have mentioned throughout the book incorporated on race day. All these points were important for my personal recovery, success, and training. All the points that helped me through my training were points that led me to success on race day. This process truly is a journey. There are going to be great moments, and there are going to be moments that are not so great. A friend once told me about this whole experience, "If you win the race, this will be a great story. If you finish the race, this will be a good story." Well, it is a good story!

Recognize accomplishments. If you can put yourself down, you will. You need to help keep yourself motivated. Every accomplishment is a good accomplishment and an important one. Give yourself credit, and keep yourself moving forward. It will always be up to you.

CHAPTER 9

Not Satisfied

I do the very best I know how, the very best I can;
and I mean to keep on doing it until the end.

–Abraham Lincoln

EVEN THOUGH I recognized the value of my accomplishment, I was very dissatisfied with my mental performance during the race. I felt it was important to do another triathlon just to prove I could fight through the race instead of fighting not to quit. My next race was much smaller, about 550 racers. I did a shorter distance, a sprint triathlon instead of an Olympic.

I approached the race as three races: the swim, the bike, and run.

When I first got in the water, this exact thought went through my head: *What are you doing here?* The thought was as clear as if I had said them out loud! I thought, *Just put your head down and go. All you need to do is the swim.* I did the swim, and when I got out, I ran to the transition area. I was determined to finish the race. I got on my bike and took off. This was actually the first time I had people really passing me on the bike, which actually encouraged me. I passed a woman who was seventy-five years old (ages are marked on the calf). As I rode by, I yelled, "You go, girl!" I whipped through the bike, and even though a few people passed me, I stayed steady the whole time. When I got back from the bike, I started the run.

I did not want to run. I had to talk my way through this leg. I was angry and trash-talking myself, and no matter how slow, I was running the whole race! I actually passed a couple people and tossed encouraging words their way: "You can do it," "Almost halfway," "Almost there," etc. I finished the race, thirteenth in my age group. I would have been in the top 10 had I ran better. After the race, I told a friend of mine, "I'm not sure why I am doing this." I had to fight my mind every bit of the way. I told him about my experience in the water and not even wanting to start the race.

Here is probably the most important thing I learned over this last year's journey. At this point, it appears I will have to fight for every step I take forward. With alcoholics, they have to always fight not to take a drink. Their mind tells them it is okay and they can have one drink. I will have to always fight going back to the couch, or so it appears so far. I mentioned earlier about the wagon moving uphill, but I want to explain it again in more depth.

Recovery is a wagon on a hill. The wagon is either going up the hill or rolling down the hill. There are no plateaus; there are no breaks, no stopping points. There are just two directions, up or down. I think this is very true for those who are fighting to regain their lives. It is and will be a constant battle. You are either going up the hill or flying back down it. You need to be prepared for this truth, because I am about to talk about my third race, and the struggle inside continues.

Thought for the Chapter

Recovery will be a constant battle. Do not be discouraged. It does get easier, from what I can tell. However, it will never be as easy as being on the couch. The couch is where you are comfortable, and it is easy. There is no responsibility, no accountability, no expectations, and it takes no effort. However, you are already taking big steps to success by reading this book. You are moving your life forward. Every step you take is an important one. Remember, you are in the wagon on a hill. You have the power to determine which direction you will be moving.

CHAPTER 10

The Next Race

When our mind and heart aren't working together, one
can always talk the other into quitting. Get your mind and
heart working together, and you will find your soul.

–A Friend

S O WHY KEEP racing? You should be asking this question. I know I have asked myself this several times. If you have not asked this question yet, I promise that you will at some point. I think it is about continuing to overcome the couch addiction and changing into something more. It does not have to be a lot more but something more.

My third race was the Portland Freshwater. *Freshwater* is a relative term as the swim was in the Willamette River. To many people, it was a disgusting river, full of pollution and other nasty items foreign to the natural mountain streams of the northwest. Compared to the Hudson, it was a breath of fresh air!

This race was different at the start. I didn't ask, Why am I here? I seemed to know the answer. I still looked at this as three distinct races, and I may look at all triathlons this way. The swim was easy. I was comfortable, confident, and moving along in a rhythmic fashion. Swimming against the current presented little challenge, and it seemed I was out of the water with a good time.

I got through the transition and started on the bike. The bike was a slight uphill grade, nothing real tough, but I definitely knew I was riding uphill. About four miles into the ride, I notice other riders dropping their gears as we started into a corner. When I came around the corner, I quickly realized why–it looked like it was going straight up. I thought, *Are you kidding me!* I started the slow, arduous grind. About halfway, I thought, *This is crap*, and I hopped off my bike. I stood there for a few moments. Again, I thought, *What am I doing?*

The struggle in my mind continues to amaze me. I'm sharing it with you because I want you to know it is coming. I want you to expect it! I want you to think about how you will get through it, around it, or over it. Know it is coming and have a plan! Jim Rohn said, "Motivation is what gets you started and habit is what keeps you going." I believe Aristotle had this in mind when he said, "We are what we repeatedly do. Excellence then is not an act, but a habit." I have been in the habit of doing nothing, expecting nothing, and asking nothing of myself. The couch or life of complacency had become my habit, and it takes a lot to change what we find to be comforting and easy.

I climbed back on my bike in the midst of what looked to be the biggest hill I had ever seen. Starting in the midst of a hill is no easy task with clip-in pedals. I would have had fewer struggles if I had not given in and continued to push. Either way, I found myself at the top of the hill, which was followed by an invigorating and somewhat scary downhill ride. For the race, we did the bike portion as a loop that had to be done twice.

I followed the lead of others and dropped my bike gears before rounding the corner. I came around the corner knowing the hill was there and had nearly the same response, "Are you kidding me!" The difference was, I didn't stop. I pushed through, remembering the downhill that wasn't all that far away. I think I will always enjoy the downhill a little more than the uphill!

The last part to the race was next, the run. The run has really been my nemesis through the entire process of triathlon racing and training. I don't excel at running. It is at the end of the race, when my body is already tired, and it is easy to convince myself to quit. I say this because we will all find an adversary along the way of recovering. I think it is good to know what that nemesis is so you can conquer it in one way or another.

I talked myself through the run. It was slow, hard, and I complained in my mind the whole way. As I neared the finish, I just had to walk. I remember taking my first step, and my coach, Richard, came running up from behind–he was in the race too. "Let's go! Pick it up! No walking here!" I literally had taken one step, and just that quickly, the quit was gone, and I ran to the finish of the race.

Thought for the Chapter

The main point I want you to take away from this chapter is our habits. Really, our life is a series of habits. We do many of the same things day after day without much thought. Sitting on the couch really didn't take much thought; it was something I did. No matter how frustrated or how saddened I became, I continued to do the same thing. Because we find comfort in doing the same things over and over, it becomes another roadblock to our success. Some of us have had the same habits for many, many years; others maybe not so long. Or maybe a tragic event has started us on a path of bad habits. I believe *insanity* can be defined as "doing the same thing over and over but expecting a different outcome" (Einstein)–this is addiction! I expect it will take at least as long, if not twice as long, to change my habits. I literally spent five years sitting on the couch. My expectation is that I will fight changing this habit to my new habit for at least five years. So in repeating Aristotle, "We are what we repeatedly do. Excellence then is not an act, but a habit." Excellence is meeting our own expectations for ourselves. Excellence is changing our negative behavior to positive behavior that allows us to move forward. Excellence is one step today, maybe two steps tomorrow, then maybe one step back and one step forward. Excellence is making a change to move your life forward.

CHAPTER 11

Lessons Learned

Where your standing changes the view, we have
the ability to change our view, just take a step
forward or to either side and look again.

–LF

I BELIEVE THIS WHOLE book is about lessons learned. If I have encouraged one person to get off the couch and make a change, then taking the time to write this book has been worthwhile. As I continue forward, there are lessons I continue to learn that help me grow in every way. I have continued to train; it has been over two years now. I completed the New York City Triathlon again with the new CNN Fit Nation group in 2011. Though the triathlon in 2011 was a better experience in many ways, looking back, the first triathlon had the biggest impact in my life.

Many of the struggles outlined in this book continue to come into my mind. These mental struggles lead to poor eating days and missed training days, and sometimes they make my training days more work then fun. However, I stay encouraged with the progress (even when it is slow) that I recognize through mental strength, changes in my attitude, and my physical changes.

I still have some days when I probably take more steps backward then forward, but I will never give up again. At the end of each day, I reflect on my accomplishments. I acknowledged my positive steps forward, think about where I can improve tomorrow, then give thanks for the day. I find this helps me to prepare for tomorrow's new challenges.

I am encouraged to my core every time I meet someone trying to change his or her life. I tell them my story to try to encourage them. When I look at how much weight I have lost, the changes in my physical appearance, the size of clothes, and my better health and attitude, I am amazed. I am able to look at things in a much more positive light. When I have a bad day, I always know tomorrow is right around the corner and it is going to be a better day.

With eight triathlons under my belt, I guess I am a triathlete. To many people outside my life, being a triathlete means swimming, biking, and running as a single event. Realistically, for me, being a triathlete means I prepare my attitude mentally, do what I need to physically, and stay off the couch. I do these three events every day! For 2012 my hope is to compete in an Ironman. The task seems daunting, but at one time, so did putting on a pair of walking shoes and heading out the door. If I can do it, you can do it. It takes the desire to change, baby steps, the desire to leave your mark, and recognizing your accomplishments then move your life forward. Once you start, never look back!

CHAPTER 12

Principles to Success

I HAVE COMPILED THE main points of success that I learned over the past two years. These are all the points talked about throughout this book. I have made them into a quick-read version so you can put them anywhere and everywhere to remind you of your journey. I look back at them now and can see where I was, where I am, and where I am going. I hope you find them helpful.

Ten Principles to Success

1. Misery does love company, so be careful whom you invite to your pity party.

2. Only you can change your life. It is your decision to go backward, stay where you are or move forward.

3. This journey is a process. The process will be filled with numerous steps—some big, some small, some backward, but in the end, most of them forward.

4. It's okay to have long-term goals, but focus on short-term goals, which may be more reasonable and attainable.

5. This is a journey, not a trip. You will need to develop good habits and not rely on gimmicks.

6. This will not be easy, so be prepared for bad moments as well as good ones. Preparation leads to success.

7. Nobody likes to be called out. Find a way to hold yourself accountable.

8. Develop a mind-set for success. (Everyone's successes will be different).

9. Recognize all of your accomplishments, big and small. If you can put yourself down, you will. You need to help keep yourself up.

10. This is a forever battle. In other words, be prepared to fight it forever. Your wagon is either slowly going

uphill or rolling downhill at a high rate of speed. It is really that simple.

The next chapter . . .

Things being as they are, the Ironman had come and gone in the time it took for this book to be published, so I decided to add the chapter that follows.

CHAPTER 13

The Ironman

That high station in life is achieved when we go through appalling situations with gallantry and grace. Frederick Buechner

S O, WHAT IS the Ironman? Most people think about Hawaii and a bunch of really thin crazy people swimming in the ocean, bicycling uphill, and running across the black volcanic pathway with temperatures over one hundred degrees.

The Ironman is partly what I mentioned above, but it is a triathlon. Many describe it as the ultimate triathlon event. The race is a 2.4-mile open water swim followed by 112-mile bicycle ride. This is all capped off with a marathon—yes, a 26.2-mile run. This all has to be done in less than seventeen hours, with times along the way for each stage. Many people will tell you it is the swim that separates triathletes from other athletes. Many say the Ironman starts at the marathon. I guess it depends on what you see as your strength in an event such as this. This race is a daunting task!

I remember that when I first thought about participating in the Ironman, it was exhilarating and intimidating at the same time. I knew I would need some friends in my camp on this one. Essentially, it was a year of training—would my body hold up? Would I hold up mentally? This is an event that takes everything you have, but do I have *it*?

I had already spent a lot of time swimming and cycling. Running, I don't care much for, but I had done my share. The injuries I've had from training mostly come from running. With the different injuries that I already had, running seemed to be the most painful, so I would substitute the elliptical machine often. The downside with the elliptical? Boredom.

For the first few months, the training wasn't much different than my normal training. The main difference was the weather going into the winter. Oregon winters are not conducive to triathlon training. Yet rain, snow, hail, wind . . .

whatever the weather, I was out there. I would tell myself, "You want to be an iron man, this is what iron men do!" On two different days, I was caught in hailstorms while riding my bike. With no shelter around, I found these two days to be the worst. Hail on a bike does not feel very good. Whatever your bike speed, you have little balls of ice bouncing off you at that speed–not my best day.

I didn't mind the snow and cold. It is more about having the right gear. I found twenty-eight degrees to be the line. Better to be inside than outside then. Some of the cool mornings were the best–the sun breaking through over the horizon; crisp, fresh air; no one else around. It took my mind off the cold, tiredness, and any aches or pains. I felt blessed just to be able to be out and exercising. In 2012, I believe I put nearly 8,500 miles on my bicycle, many of them in the rain and weather.

As time neared, I was excited and scared to death all at the same time. There were days that were completely consumed with self-doubt. I needed more time to train. I could never do this. My favorite: *What was I thinking?* I would try to be confident in all the days I had trained. Some days, my training days would suffer as I talked myself into thinking, *What is the point? It was out of my reach anyway!* Remember, my goal is to finish the race within seventeen hours, which means sixteen hours, and fifty-nine minutes was my goal time.

More than self-doubt, I had days filled with moments of terror. I mean, such a deep fear it was terror. I was going to drown, crash my bike, die from heat exhaustion, or have a heart attack. The irrationality of the fear was obvious, but I had never experienced anything like this. The fear was real and impacted me in many ways. People would ask how I was doing during my preparation. I would tell them, "Nervous with moments of pure terror." They would laugh as if I were being sarcastic, but I had never been more serious. In all the moments of my life, I had never experienced more emotion, fear, self-doubt, and excitement as I did in the month leading up to the Ironman. I told a friend of mine, "You want to experience life? Sign up for an Ironman!" There was no doubt that I was alive, never more alive. I was aware of every emotion, every fear, every physical weakness I had ever known.

When I flew to Kentucky, the flight took forever. The flight was filled with athletes headed to the Ironman. They were carrying their Ironman garb and gear from previous races. It seemed like I was going to be the only rookie. Everyone looked so fit, determined, and ready. Even though

I had lost a substantial amount of weight, I did not see myself looking as fit as the other athletes. My coach told me, "Your eye is going to go to the most fittest people there, and it will start to take away from your confidence. You will start to think you have no business being there. But Ironman athletes come in all shapes and sizes. You need to fight this thought and feeling." She said, "I don't know why this happens, but it does." That was exactly what I needed to hear as that was exactly what I was experiencing, and it was tearing down my confidence minute by minute.

My friend told me, "You are not competing against anyone there. You are competing against your own time . . . This is your race." Honestly, I had so much encouragement from friends, acquaintances, and people whom I worked with and trained with that it probably enabled me to make the trip to Kentucky. Without all the support and encouragement, I'm not sure I would have had the courage to board the plane.

Though all the advice and well wishes were helpful, one of the best pieces of advice (even though I didn't get to use it) I received was this: "Run each mile of the marathon for someone that means something to you . . . Save the last mile for your brother." Another person I talked with who is a four-time Ironman said this: "The first race is about finishing. The second race is about feeling like you're going to live when you finish. The third race is about your time."

When I arrived at the host hotel for the Ironman, all I can say is, it was amazing. There was so much excitement and enthusiasm in the air. Everything seemed larger than life. The bicycles, athletes, flyers, volunteers . . . everything! It was simply breathtaking. I walked down to the transition area–Ironman stuff everywhere! I could envision the race as I looked out over the endless Ohio River. The river was so big! Huge bridges spanned the river, which was slow moving, peaceful, and oh yeah, huge! I couldn't believe how big the river was. I could see where we would exit the river and head into the transition area. I could see where you left transition on the bike, then back in, only to turn around and run out. There was a huge bridge that joined Kentucky to Indiana stretching over the Ohio River and providing shade to the transition area. This was the first leg of the run, across the bridge and back. I thought, *I had never been to* Indiana. What a way to get there.

I went back to the hotel and put my bike together. I took it for a test ride, going about eight miles of the bike route then back. I didn't want to work too hard before the race. The day was simply amazing–I was at the Ironman, it is the world's greatest race, and in a few days, I would be participating. I had no doubt that I would finish the race. I thought of how incredible it was to be there and how far I had come. I looked around at all the people who would be competing and wondered what their story might be. Everyone has a reason for showing up at the Ironman.

The next couple of days, I walked to the transition area a million times if I did once. I studied where I would come out of the water after swimming 2.4 miles. I would see where I would enter the transition area, pick up my gear, then go to the changing tent. Where I would need to go to get my bike, then run out of the transition to start the grueling 112-mile bike ride in the Kentucky heat. I studied where I would come back, pick up my gear, and get back to the changing tent then back out the other side to start the run toward the bridge that spanned the Ohio River. I feel like I am going on and on about this, but it was so amazing. It is one of those moments you will never forget in your life no matter how long you live.

Sunday morning, it all started. I got up at 3:00 a.m. to be certain I was good and awake at race time. I had packed everything I needed the night before, which seemed pointless since I unpacked everything the next morning, and then packed it again. I headed to the transition area. I wanted to be there at 5:00 a.m. There were people everywhere. It was like no one had slept. I checked my bike and my tire pressure, put my water bottles in their cages, and added my flat tire kit. Everything looked right. I believed I was ready to go.

Then the walk–the mile-and-a-half walk to the starting line. It was crazy walking down the sidewalk in the dark of the night with three thousand of my closest Ironmen friends and all of their friends. I felt a bit like a lemming, not really sure where I was going but just following everyone else in the pitch-black of the night. There was a definite hush. It was amazing how so many people walking could be so quiet.

Once I got to the starting line, I had to walk at least another half mile to get to the end of the line. There were so many people, all going through different rituals as they prepared for the twelve-hour journey that is the Ironman. I stood for a couple of hours. The cameraperson for CNN showed up and interviewed me. I really was not all that nervous, or maybe I was just too scared to say much. It was really too late to look back now.

The race began with a time trial start, two people every five seconds until all three thousand people were in the water. Once the line started moving forward, it moved fast. Quickly it was my turn–even if I wanted to change my mind, it was too late. Before I knew it, I was jumping off the dock and into the Ohio River to start my Ironman journey. This section of the Ironman was 2.4 miles of open water swimming.

The open water swim is a full contact event! But before the throw-down started, I was swimming in the incredibly calm and warm water of the Ohio. We were in a cove area, so there were boats moored off to my right. I could see them every time I took a breath. One of my friends had told me to enjoy the moment and remember everything. He wanted to hear about the depth and breadth of my experience. As I was trying to get myself calm, lower my heart rate, and slow my breathing, I started getting into the groove of my swim.

I did a quick spot for the directional buoys to make sure I was on track. On the right I could see a large boat called the *Linda Kay*. It made me laugh to myself. When I spotted forward, I could see the sun breaking through the horizon. It was beautiful! There was an orange-and-yellow glow with an illumination of warmth. The rising sun was a bright beacon leading the swimmers in the direction of the finish line, assisted by a few fluffy white clouds. I felt calm as I thought about my friend's words to enjoy the moment then began to settle into my swim stroke. I smiled to myself, since a real smile would have meant swallowing water. I'd look at the sunrise every moment I could. It was calming and warming like a halo. I thought, *This is the greatest day ever!*

As I approached the first turn buoy, around eight hundred meters, the sun wasn't near as spectacular as it had been. The swim had become a full-contact sport. Instead of swimming to finish the race, I found myself swimming to stay alive. One of the competitors hit me so hard at the buoy my goggles came down off my face, and I was certain I would have a black eye. As the race continued, I found myself being hit and kicked moment by moment. Other people were swimming across my legs, pushing them down in the water, forcing me to pull harder with my upper body to stay afloat. They would swim over the top of my legs, the top of me, or hit me with their arm stokes. This became my least favorite part of the race. I found myself becoming angered by the fact that people would choose to swim over the top of me or were content to hit or kick me over and over.

As things slowed down and the full-contact part of the swim minimized, I began getting some cramps in my legs, which worried me a bit. They would seem to work out then come back. They weren't bad, but they were a reminder that I had been in the water for a good period of time. Two point four miles in the water is hard to quantify since most of my swimming was in a pool. I could see a bridge up ahead, only to realize it wasn't the bridge near the finish. The next bridge, the same thing—it wasn't the bridge I was hoping for. I remember thinking, *When is this ever going to end!* It ended eventually. I remember grabbing the hand of a volunteer near the stairs as I came out of the water and onto the stairway. This is not an easy task, by the way. Your body has been horizontal for so long, it takes a bit to get used to being vertical again.

As the blood rushed around in my body and I started to get my balance, I felt good. One down, one to go—even though there were two stages to go, I prefer to look at the triathlon as three separate races and I take one race at a time. So in my mind, just the bike was next. As I mentioned, I felt good. I ran the length to the transition area, got my gear, and headed out on my bike.

I really felt good on the bike. According to my computer, I was averaging twenty to twenty-three miles per hour. I was passing people like crazy. I kept telling myself to slow down; I had a long ride ahead. According to the Ironman timing information, I passed three hundred people in the first twenty miles. I remember thinking, *Wooo whooo!* but I kept telling myself to slow down.

I stayed right on track with my plan, nutrition, salt tabs, electrolytes, etc. It was really hot out, above ninety. I could feel the heat, so I was really focused on my plan. At about forty miles, I started to feel dizzy, a little disoriented–not bad, just unsettled. I thought it was dehydration. I had stuck to my plan, so it didn't make sense. I added more water. I stepped up my next nutrition and salt stop by fifteen minutes. I didn't feel any better–if anything, a little worse.

At forty-five miles, I got an unbelievable cramp in my left leg. My leg was bent, and I could literally see the muscle pulsating. It was excruciating. I couldn't straighten my leg. I had to clip out of my pedal and stop. I couldn't get my leg all the way straight. I started rubbing it and trying to stretch it. Finally, the muscle loosened and let my leg straighten. It still hurt like crazy. I thought, *What is this about?* After about ten minutes, my leg felt near normal and just had a sore spot in it. I got back on my bike and continued on.

At about fifty miles, it happened again. This was even worse, if it could be. I started to dry-heave, and I struggled to clip out of my pedal and come to stop. This time I had to stand for about twenty minutes before my leg started working again. I looked at my time. I was doing everything right. I thought for sure I was dehydrated. When I was able to get back on my bike, I was just a few miles from the aid station. I stopped, got off my bike, drank a whole bottle of Gatorade, and covered my head and neck with cool water. The only thing that was on my mind was dehydration and heat exhaustion, although that didn't make sense. I kept thinking back–I was about five hours into the race, and I had done everything just as I had planned. After stopping for a good fifteen minutes, I got back on my bike. At about mile 55, my right leg locked in the straight position. I couldn't move it, and I couldn't pedal my bike. Worse, I couldn't clip out. As the bike started slowing, it was obvious I was going to fall over. I kept trying to unclip my pedal. My leg was cramped so badly tears were rolling down my face from the pain. Mostly, I didn't want to fall over on the bike. At the last second, I was able to move my heel enough to get the pedal unlocked. I stood there for a few minutes, my heart pounding. My leg was excruciating! It seemed like I could see the muscles pulsating like I had seen on the other leg. I couldn't get control of the muscle to bend my leg.

As I stood there rubbing my leg, I noticed another rider off the road. He was bent over, vomiting. I asked him if he was all right. (During the briefing for the Ironman, they tell us to check on one another if things don't seem right.) He didn't answer me, but he was bent over, vomiting, and his bike lay on the ground. I could tell he was in bad shape. I asked again if he was all right, and he didn't respond. I asked him if he needed medical help, and he told me yes. Since no one else was asking, I thought I had best get on my way to get him help.

The next five miles were the slowest of my life. I thought, *This poor guy. He has the slowest rider out here going for help.* I kept watching people ride by me, thinking any one of these guys could get him help faster than me. My legs hurt so bad I was still dizzy, but I had no more dry heaves. I got to the next aid station and gave the people the information and bib number of the rider and called my own race.

I was so disappointed. At this point, it is hard to tell if it was disappointment or the pain in my legs that kept me quiet, but I didn't want to talk to anyone. I thought, *They should make me walk back!* After waiting around for a while, I and about fifteen others got into what I call "the bus of shame." It was a long ride on the bus of shame. Everyone was having different discussions. Two others on this bus had experienced what seemed to be a similar sodium deficiency. One of the riders had done four prior Ironmans and never experienced this before. I guess this made me feel a little better, but not really.

Another rider was talking with me, trying to encourage me. It just kept going through my mind that I was on the bus of shame. As I listened to everyone talk, I sat quiet. The bus ride was so long, but then again, we were sixty miles out from the start.

When the bus of shame dropped us at the transition area, we had to give them our timing chips. This was the ending to my Ironman. Then the bus pulled away, and I stood in a parking lot about fifty feet from all the spectators. My friends and the CNN cameraman were walking to where I was. I remember huge tears rolling down my face under my sunglasses. I had a lot of thoughts about this race–not finishing or not finishing like this was not one of them. I just wanted to walk away and not face anyone. The disappointment and feeling like I had let everyone down were almost overwhelming. I had to make some phone calls and let people who were following me online know that I was out of the race so they wouldn't worry. I called my best friend and said I was out of the race. I said, "There is nothing you can say in this moment that will make this moment okay." I hung up the phone. I started getting a ton of text messages asking me what had happened and if I was okay. I didn't have the heart to return any of them. I did my interview with CNN then grabbed my stuff and went down the "walk of shame" back to the hotel. It is just hard to explain the disappointment and disbelief. Of all the scenarios in my head, this was not one of them. I thought I would not finish due to timing out (not meeting the seventeen hours), but not quitting.

Of course, all of my friends were trying to encourage me and tell me it was okay and I had done great. I understood that in some ways, but none of it was consoling. I'm not sure if I felt that I had let others down or had just let myself down. All the time, all the training, everything for nearly a year focused around this race. How did it get so big? Why did it mean so much? Oh, and my legs hurt so bad! A friend of mine sent me a text saying, "There is always next year." I remember replying, "Not for me!" He said, "Don't say that now. We will talk later!"

Through my disappointment, I knew logically that it was a blessing to have just shown up. Two and a half years ago, I could have never dreamed of being at an Ironman. When I think about the eighty-five pounds I lost, I can't even imagine getting on my bike and strapping on an eighty-five-pound weight. I can't imagine running with an eighty-five-pound backpack, so that in itself is a victory.

It is not just about the weight but the wellness of my body physically, mentally, and spiritually. I was no longer on pain medication. I didn't have the daily pain mentally or physically. Honestly, the weight of my life had changed so dramatically in the last two years that these are the things I need to focus on. Pity parties are no longer a standard for me. I am a person of courage and physical, mental, and spiritual strength, and that is what I always need to be.

Even with that in mind, the next few days were difficult. I didn't want to bring my bike back home. I didn't want to see anyone I knew. I didn't want to go back to work. I didn't wear anything on the plane that indicated I had been at the Ironman. My biggest hope was that no one would ask me questions. It is a long flight from Kentucky to Oregon; I had a lot of time to think about the Ironman over and over and over.

Without a doubt, to this day and this very moment, I would have preferred to finish the Ironman. With all I've experienced over the last six years, it seems easy to forget the very lesson I want to share with everyone: the experience of inspiration, motivation, and life-changing experiences that we encounter every day.

The blessing really is to have had the opportunity to show up. As days went by, I really do feel deep in my soul that the ability to train, show up, and be on the starting line is a big part of the Ironman. Really, it isn't even about the Ironman. It is about making the decision to prepare and show up for any and all experiences that come our way. It is always easier not to prepare. It is easier to not show up. It is easier to ride the bus of shame and never get off. Though I still feel disappointment at times, I really, truly understand the big picture.

Thought for the Chapter

The big picture is what I want to share with anyone who will listen. It really isn't about the destination but the journey. It really isn't about how many breaths we take but how many moments that take our breath away. It is about the breadth and depth of each moment we experience. It is about taking what we learn and letting it make us stronger instead of shaking our foundation. It is about not hiding from the tornado but standing on the roof and letting the tornado give you rock-star hair! We set the expectations! We decide what we learn from our journeys. We decide which experiences, good or bad, we will learn from, and we decide the impact we let those things have on our lives. As I mentioned earlier in this book, we are wagons on our hills. We are either traveling up at a slow, deliberate, and continuous pace, or we are coming down at a high rate of speed.

The next race was probably more important for so many reasons. A few weeks after the Ironman, I went to Malibu, California, to meet up with the new CNN Fit Nation group. Remember, this is where I got my start, so what a great place to go back to after my race in Kentucky! This weekend recentered me! This race reminded me where I had been and how far I had come. Watching the new group, "the lucky seven," finish the race, the emotion and the sense of accomplishment was incredible. The ability to transform your life path and accomplish something that really didn't seem possible. Then taking the accomplishments as an opportunity to inspire others and helping them to beat their own couch addiction.

When I first arrived at Malibu, I met up with the CNN producers. It was amazing to see them. I felt so grateful inside for the opportunity they had provided. Without the opportunity, I might not have had the fortitude to move forward. The Malibu race was a good race. It wasn't a great race in terms of speed or time; I still had the fatigue and soreness from the Ironman a few weeks prior. But it was a great race in terms of lessons learned and my lifetime journey. The race took me back to where I had started. It reminded me of the blessing it is to be where I am. It reminded me of where I once was but don't ever want to be again. It reminded me that it isn't always about finishing the race–sometimes it is just about showing up at the starting line.

CPSIA information can be obtained
at www.ICGtesting.com
Printed in the USA
BVHW030848020519
547058BV00023B/65/P